MW01713401

ROBERT LIMA

RAMÓN DEL VALLE-INCLÁN

ODYSSEY

Floricanto Press

Floricanto Press

7177 Walnut Canyon Rd.

Moorpark, California 93021

(415) 793-2662

www. *FloricantoPress*. com

ISBN-13: 978-1-951088-17-0

LCNN: 2021930369

"*Por nuestra cultura hablarán nuestros libros. Our books shall speak for our culture.*"

Roberto Cabello-Argandoña, Editor

ROBERT LIMA

RAMÓN DEL VALLE-INCLÁN

O D Y S S E Y

POETRY AND PROSE

Acknowledgments

I am indebted to Dr. Archie Allen, the then Chair of the Classics Department at Penn State University, who invited me to compile and read the prose and poetry herein at the Classics Symposium in conjunction with The Year of Homer in 1991. This is a wholly revised, illustrated version of that presentation.

Among the poems in *Odyssey* are some that were first published in the following periodicals: *Broadside, Delta Epsilon Sigma Bulletin, Dorna (Spain), Dreamworks, Images, The Literary*

Review, Lyra, Paunch, Pivot; others were published in the books *Fathoms, The Olde Ground, The Pointing Bone, Tracking the Minotaur, Self, Celestials, Anthology of Magazine Verse and Yearbook of American Poetry, Elementals, (Borges) Simply a Man of Letters, Erato & Noima Magazine* (Greece).

For Stavros Girgenis,

who translated & published many of these poems into Greek.

PREFATORY NOTE

My immediate touchstones for this selection of my poems are Homer, the legendary author of the *Iliad* and the *Odyssey*, other writings attributed to the blind bard, and the broad Greek tradition of antiquity.

The classic world-view is expanded herein by the insightful words of Ramón del Valle-Inclán (Spain, 1866-1936) on the traditions and beliefs of ancient Greece. They, too, are touchstones for this collection.

The prose texts that introduce the collection and accompany the poems are from *The Lamp of Marvels* (Lindisfarne Press, 1986), my translation of *La lámpara maravillosa* (1916) by Ramón del Valle-Inclán.

Here, in *Odyssey*, two modern writers assess the Greek Way of myths and folklore in prose and poetry. The illustrations throughout enhance the words.

PROPULAION: THE GREEKS OF ANTIQUITY

"Their souls were filled with sacred paths leading to groves, crystalline brooks, grottoes out of which flew long-winged birds at twilight, the shadows of laurels, and distant, golden shores of a blue sea. With eyes open in amazement to the light, they received all images as if they were the eucharistic species, images so frequent and diverse that they summed up the norms of all knowledge.

The perception of the Greeks was the child of the sea and sky, of hills with olive groves and vineyards, of mountains with their herds, of forests with their spirits, and of the lustiness of forms.

The varying images their eyes took in while traveling rustic paths gave agility to body and mind. They did not receive their understanding of the world like a cold inheritance from the urn of words—always a lengthy, obscure, chronological, and gross mode of knowledge. To those herdsmen, ideas meant numbers and forms under the rhythm of the Sun. Whenever they reposed on the heights, looking into the depth of tilled, verdant and intense valleys, they felt the mystical emotion of oneness.

Those mythic Greeks, having ploughed the brown lap of the plain and known each path as well as a long tale, became center and consciousness of vision upon the heights. And every star-filled night, while gathered around the bonfire and feeling the breath of the sleeping herd, they felt the exaltation of recalling images of the day and reliving them in the tales of the older herdsmen.

What they learned impulsively was enjoyed in quietude."

Ramón del Valle-Inclán

ODYSSEY

I

AOIDOS

"And it was a blind minstrel, to whom night seemed eternal, who first kindled the corona of the Sun through the music of his words. Homer the Patriarch was able to give the verses the name of a flower: Helio-tropes."

SIGHT

The blind man

is the one

from whom

the universe

has been stolen

without

redress

Homer

is the seer

of the

Inner Eye

"The blind pupils of the gods in Greek marbles symbolize this supreme vision, which imprisons within a circle all that is perception."

HORIZON

where the eye sees too far

where the mind thinks too large

matter shapeless, indistinct

beyond dimension or perspective

troglodytic and extinct

like the bloody sunset

EYES

Blind man,

blind man,

the star is black

the sun extinct

the moon eclipsed

What demon

has swallowed

your light?

Blind man,

Blind man,

the star is near

the sun is harnessed

the moon is walked

What god

has stolen

your mind?

"Those who were loved by the gods in Greek antiquity were born under the star of a lamentable destiny. Fate dragged them along like a sacred wind, disheveling their souls, their garments, and their hair. Because lives convulsed with pain are the object of love, misfortune was a celestial gift."

II

S E A W A Y S

"The means are no longer needed when the end is attained, as is the case with oars and sails when a vessel reaches port."

V O Y A G E R

I

The pilot leaves the ship.

Soon, too, the open arms of land

are gone, receding in the mist

behind the wake we leave.

No gulls in flight to see us out.

Now, open sea for voyaging.

A moment's sun breaks through

to cheer our loss of land

and warm the chill of air,

but steel grey sea and sky

await our prow through daylight hours.

II

The time goes slowly while aboard.

You sit on deck chairs

seeing the horizon pass itself off

as an endless line belying curvature

and eyes take straightness as their own

through time and space.

III

Where I am
Center,
sea's horizon
circles me,
a dot
within
the dark
of night.

IV

We voyage where the ancients did,
between the continental shelf of Breizh
and island shores of Kernow, Eire,
claiming for ourselves the Celtic Sea
of Brendan and the sons of Breogan
within the navigation of a dream.

V

The gulls now come from nowhere
to play their rings astern
upon an unexpected azure sky.

Soon, land again,
the voyager to be a trekker
on yet another element.

DESCENT

Leaving the once-bright star

dissolving into barely light,

the sky into the water

limitless and dark

Seeking the depths from heights,
descending beyond tolerance
to the murky level of bottom life

Descending into fathoms,
going down through the fear.

II

THANATOPSIS

"The Greeks never knew the terror of death ... Since that time the ideas of death and life became as one in human consciousness."

TALE

Man feels his birth

the longest moment;

Man intuits death

and satisfactions.

Somewhere

in between,

the living tense,

Man hazards himself

to stir creation

and so, envisions

rounded moons and crests,

self-less chimeras,

fauvist love.

Man touches water

irreducibly.

JOURNEYER

I

look at my form

and see

its changing

patterns

. . .

addenda and

deletions

toward the cycle

of completion.

I,

observer

of the body,

a traveler

in the capsule

of the flesh,

am ready

to depart

upon this

recognition

to true

Self.

EXCARNATION

The predatory ways of nature
have been served by the exposure
of dead human flesh to elements
and carrion-eating beasts of prey.

When death has conquered life,
the corpses are left out-of-doors
to be defleshed, and when the bones
have bleached to a white state,

the skulls and other human parts
are placed for separate entombment
in the chambered lithic barrows
of the tribal burial mounds.

Ancient death-ways

strangely moving

in the give and take

of hard existence.

INTIMACY

When the wild wind slices
there's no recourse
but to let it through.

So it is that elements
enter willfully to life,
cutting full to heart.

And when the exit's made,
the evidence of wound is gone
as with the slice of wind.

PASSAGE

As dawn approaches in its quietude
dampness penetrates to bones
inspiring bone-thoughts
of a crossing
to be navigated in the dew
like Charon oaring Acheron eternally
from shore to shore
without a smile
or tear

the water of the river is sufficient
and weight is only cumbersome
in lower depths
the poet found in his travails

the simile awakens pensiveness
and forces a retreat
but momentarily
through light's own surge

AFTER AN ANONYMOUS EIGHTH-CENTURY GAELIC POET

That long and cold day in Great Moor
foreshadowed devastating nights
with rain, no trifle, lashing through
the ancient wood that sheltered life,
the clean wind howling a great roar.

The gusts had broken his resolve,
had crushed the poet's spirit with
their great, relentless icy thrusts,
had drowned him in his human plight.
He suffered endlessly in time!

To voice his sad condition to the King,
(upon the distant star-bright throne),
like Job before his deity, who lacked
a sense of human suffering or need,
he wrote the pain in "Wind" and "Storm."

The poems shout of wind consuming life
like twigs beset by raging crimson fire
ordained by Heaven for a purpose that
the poet's reason cannot quite surmise.
There was no course but deep despair.
His grief took form in plaintive words
that still describe our meager state
(a hopeless fear yet shakes the mien

when Nature's elemental powers rear).

There is no respite from the cruel wind.

DREAMSPEAKER

When this land was our land
we did not put our dead
into a hole in the ground,
their nostrils to fill with earth,
their bodies to rot with worms.

We honored their lives and
placed them high upon a tree
stretched on a wooden bier
to see the land, feel the breeze,
to be over earth, triumphant.

Death does not mean the end.

Death makes us company

with the future and the past,

as in a dream.

IV

DIONYSIA

"The laughter of fauns, the pipes of satyrs, and the dance of sylvans continue to echo through the forests, and men have never ceased to hear the immortal spirits."

REVELERS

Vital concert of the flesh's embrace

in crescendo to the lusting throes

Celebrate the primal rite

naked before open fires

rapt and swaying airily

to the riparian sound

pressing closely on the earth

to earth at night

glissando

Signature of Love

explicit tempo

swelling into brief cadenzas

at the movement's end

"Only when we lose ourselves in the musical paths of the Panic jungle can we hear the footsteps and evoke the shadow of the unknown being who accompanies us." / "Our entire Dionysiac life is pervaded with mystical intuitions!"

DANCERS

Volatile, arms flay the space,

torsos sway in rare rapidity,

legs toe earth with frictiveness.

Rhythm into cyclical resolve--

oneness in the hold--the shining

of the Pan/Daemonium in human course.

"The eroticism of Greek art discloses the *Hermetic* meaning of the Platonic ideas: It is the eternal affirmation of the future through the love which perpetuates form. ... The first aesthetic rose grows out of the theological concept of the Spermatic Logos. ... The theological conceptions of the ancients were animated by the infinite possibilities of the Spermatic Logos."

THIASOS

Upon Cithaeron,

where the lion dwelt,

the Theban women

split the night asunder
with their cries
of ecstasy
in Dionysian rites,
rending clothing
and the random body
lost to worship
of the Lord of Chaos,
letting loose
the Beast
within themselves.

V

MYTHOS

"Those who were loved by the gods in Greek antiquity were born under the star of a lamentable destiny. Fate dragged along like a sacred wind, disheveling their souls, their garments, and their hair. Because lives convulsed with pain are the object of love, misfortune was a celestial gift. If tragic heroes are perpetuated in our minds with an almost divine aspect, it is due to the compassionate shudder with which we contemplate them. ... Heroes, appearing before us as gods condemned to live the life of men, possess a humanity forged from pain."

HERACLES

He stalks his prey,

scattered like birds

and clamoring.

Heracles

draws the string

(his bow arches to his might)

but does not give release.

He is an image--

wasted, useless power--

forever looking,

a replica of his old self . . .

and *ponos*, he soon learns,

can mean both labor

and attendant pain.

Heracles,

it is impossible

to kill the dead.

IKAROS

Not on feather and wax wings

Like the ancient fliers,

Daedalus and Ikaros,

Whose joy in soaring

To salute the Sun,

The God of Light,

Led to downfall

of the son into the sea,

A vapor tail now leaves a trail

From silver wings that also

Soar across expansive sky

With upsurge threading

The element of Air

Into the plane of Sun.

VI

A G O N

"Within the esoteric scheme of tragedy, Fate is a theological grace, possesses something of the gods' breath, and girds human passions with an eternal significance. Fully covered with horror and blood, the shades of ancient fables raise their arms out of the mist of myth like spectres from our consciousness, which avidly seeks itself in all shrieks of pain and trembles on self-recognition. And in this dark instinct, which warns that under the sway of Fate all types of pain may assail us, is at the same time an aesthetic intuition."

KATHARSIS

The audience is a sea,

the stage an isle

The first

unseemly populated

by a variegated cast

astir with gestures, moves

cacophonous

before the act

The second

is devoid of life

until the waves are stilled

Then actors take their stance

and so

the play begins

The *agon* on the stage,

the one beyond the boards

together one

The island in the sea,

the tides around the shore

The parts become a whole

A TOMOS

Leucippus and Democritus

They are indivisible,
everlasting and thus,
in a persistent flow …

We lose atoms
from the moment
of our birth

and being near inert
will not suffice
to curb the flow

too soon
we will be one
with all the universe
and cease to be

the one

that we have barely

known

VII

BEING

"The primitive art of the Greeks, evocative of the eternal meaning of life, encoded the supreme comprehension of Beauty in the knowledge attained by placing the images of the world outside the context of time."

A M P H O R A

The vessel that I am contains all things.
Nothing that has been is absent from my hold.

My clay façade looks individualized
(distinct, distinguishable, apart in mode),
yet I'm an old repository filled with other times.

I am totality inside this mold, everything
that has been in the times, beyond them even,
lived, suspected, known, revealed or loved . . .
all that has existed or could be . . .

Since nothing that has been somehow in time
or out, has been deprived from me, or will,
potentially all things will be in me
(or now exist, beyond the sequitur of hours).
Even when I'm dead I will be filled.

VIII

OLYMPIANS

"The eurythmics of naked bodies vitalizes their religious and heroic myths. Apollo and Venus personify the religious longing of the procreative instinct to make the human ideal divine. ... Hellenic antiquity wandered along eternally enamored of supreme norms."

HEPHAESTUS

In ancient Hellas
it was held as deep belief
that this Olympian
made the weaponry
for all his comrades,
tempering the swords,
the lances, shields
and poniard blades
within his fiery furnace,
shaping them upon his anvil.

Hephaestus,

God of Fire,

Lord of all that came

from earth's volcanic entrails

with devastating force.

GODDESSES

1

EOS

Dawn

spirals out

from her

point of origin

to the extension

of high noon

and then,

half-lived,

turns back,

spiraling

upon itself,

to its dark

point of

dissolution

2

ARTEMIS

huntress

on the land

is she who

closes distance

to her prey,

bow and arrow

of her craft

tautly held

until release

3

HEKATE

is the

triple one

who triumphs

darkly

from her

Underworld

4

SELENE

the distant body

in the sky

is she who

rends the night

with

silver rays

like knives

SABBAT

The woman of the sky
trusts me to dream
in the diapason of rays
becoming soon a swell,
symphonic in its cadences,
a force in reverie.
Crescent goddess,
I long to be tangential
and cross horned curve
with my diameter
intimate in lunacy

ARCHETYPE

C A V E

narrow

secluded

apart from light

containment

enclosure

concealment

separate reality

concave entrance

leading to the inner

space

labyrinthine byway to

The Mother

Womb

Source

Chamber

Conch Shell

C A V E

sacral path to

The Goddess

IX

DAEMON

"The classical rose blossoms in the second circle; it is a rose of marvelous geometry, an androgynous rose, a word rose which brings together the antagonism of hours and lives in one supreme synthesis."

A V A T A R

The features
ebb and flow
with the fluidity
of tides

Limbs,
muscular, defined,
become appendages
of viscous form
spanning space
for an extended reach,

e l o n g a t e d

to gigantic terms

to meld again

into minutiae

with phenomenal resolve,

dissolving

differences into a soft

androgyny

X

KOSMOS

"The Golden Age was dawning and the Greeks, divine herdsmen, were still contemplating pale stars. They did so, enveloped in the silence of flocks, on hills dappled with olive trees, among guardian dogs. Their souls came forth at dawn; those goatherds possessed the sovereign eyes of eagles and an intuition wrenched from the celestial core of the Sun."

FOLKLORE

Sun's fiery rays
shaft through the air
to draw from land and sea
the moisture that they hold.

Once borne aloft,
the waterclouds replenish Earth
with storms and rain
when channeled beams recede.

The elemental cycle
forms a mutual bond
between all things that are
and others yet to be.

ASTRALS

"We are such stuff as
dreams are made on."
Shakespeare

We have been taught our bodies came from dust,
to dust, then, would return at death.

Tonight, I learned that only half a truth was told
for wise astronomers, as one, now state
that stardust was the matrix ore
of which all things were ultimately made
when, primally, a Supernova burst
and sprinkled its debris across
the far-flung galaxy that's our abode.

Since then, our bodies, made of astral dust,
are longing to locate themselves once more
among the womb of stars.

NAKED SINGULARITIES

If they exist, they shake some underpinnings of
the cosmic theory set by Einstein,
ideas on matter, gravity, as well as
space and time--the relativity of each to each.

Naked singularities may be resultants of
gigantic clouds of particles collapsing on themselves,
their regions near the pointed ends
condensing into areas infinite in density and weight.

There is grave danger in all this for Nature
is believed unable to produce such dire effects,
create a force that has no bounds, is infinite,
and, naked, lies beyond the gravity black holes contain,

themselves perceived to be, but still unproved.
The singularities that may exist therein are clothed,

but yet they are unable to communicate their selves
for nothing in black holes can reach our ken

and anything approaching their serenity would find
its very being wrenched and torn to shreds.
Indeed "There are more things in heaven and earth
than are dreamt of in our philosophy," or Einstein's,

and the dilemma of "To be or not to be" takes on
significance beyond the existential stage of man on Earth
when naked singularities that had no possibility of life
intrude upon the very fabric of the Universe's sense.

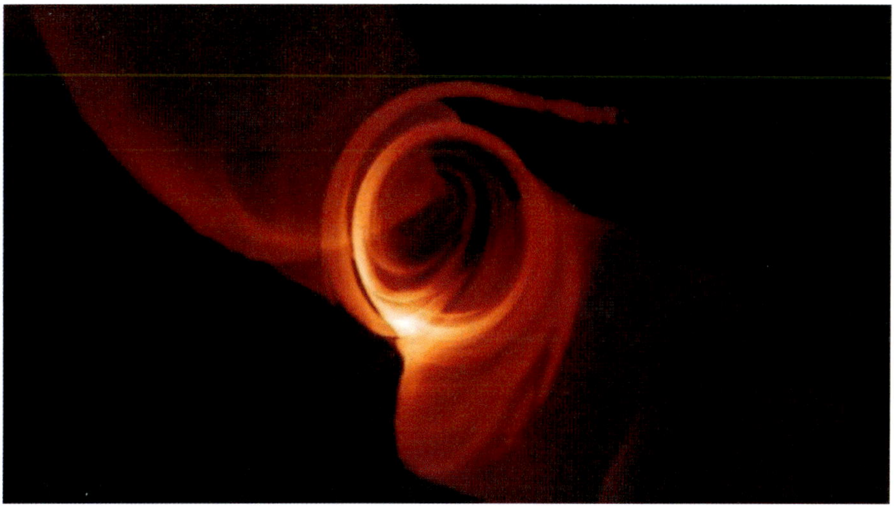

XI

MONSTERS

"The Platonic Ideas are intuitions of aesthetic quietism. ... The Hellene filled the mythological forests of his golden isles with centaurs. (He) combined the shapes, but no one created them. ... The monsters of Byzantine art, wherein primal forms degenerate into absurdity, teach us this comprehension of Beauty in opposition to Hellenism, which perpetuates the eternal sense of life in the ideas of Plato. Gargoyles, corbels, dragons, beasts of fantastic mien had this new intuitiveness ensconced in their perverse forms; their character, elaboration of uniqueness, was set against the archetype by which the ancient world had set its course. ... The poet combines them, assembles them, and using known elements also invents a lineage of monsters: his own."

BESTIARY

Ancient monsters,

degenerate and wild,

adorn the pages

in the exercise

of matter overcome

by mind's imaginings,

decadent with hard

illusions,

rampant stratagems

Behind the Beast

there lies the Beauty

that all things possess.

AL ANDER HERSCHAFT IST VON GOT
ZVR HVLF DEM MENSCHEN IN DER NOT
ON SATAN VNDT SEIN BERSTLICH ROT
SEINDT HERNIV STIFTEN SVNDT VNDT TODT
DER BABST HEIST RECHT DER WILDEMAN
DER DVRCH SEIN FALSCHES SCHALCKES BAN
AL VNGLVCK HAT GERICHTET AN
DAS GOT VNDT MENSCHEN NICHT LEIDEN KAN
1545
MART LVTHER D
SINDT DIE HERN

ORCUS

Ursus once, my name became as one
with giants for my awesome size;
and then in victims' minds of yore
I came to be the legendary Wild Man
of a nightmare's fearsome stint.

Orcus now, I bear his ragged badge.
Dressed in the tatterdemalion
of dead leaves and twigs,
lichen and multi-colored tufts
of hairy fur, I wander through

the forests of the alpine heights
and in the regions far below,
my nature metamorphosed, become
a freakish thing that's not akin to
mien of either beast or man.

There is a mask of ebon on my face
that hints at darker things beneath
the hirsute aspect and the craggy brow:
the tremors that the mind instills,
the horror of a night unstilled . . .
Uprooting massive trees, I bear them
on my giant shoulders with the ease
of one accustomed to such brutish feats,
the massive strength of Ursus being one
with that of Orcus in my wild dichotomy.

I sojourn with the walking dead,
wailing to the tall Tyrolean night.
I lead the Wild Horde through the pace,
an endlessly telluric Dance of Death.
My face and bearing terrify the land.

Captive in a quandary of ancient lore,
I am the Wild Man of the darkest thoughts,
haunted, hunted now by others who pursue
their very own exotic dream through me
In time of Carnival. I am the brute they seek.

INCUBUS

Magic being out of woodland bowers--
faun, or satyr, woodwose, sylvan,
beast--hirsute daemon out of time,
evil reaper of the restless night,
vile seducer of the female flesh . . .

Thus, Merlin came to be from savage love,
unwary maiden taken in Bretagne's wood,
Brocéliande, by Incubus in satyr's guise.
The hellish plan to breed the Anti-Christ
within that virgin's womb was foiled
by her true virtue, which entwined in him
along with powers preternatural and wild
that helped the kingdom Arthur ruled.
But other offspring did not fare as well.
For women having carnal knowledge of a man
beyond the confines of the wedded state
who found themselves in dire fertility
did vow that Incubus had lain with them
through mists of troubled, nightmare sleep.
Exempt from knowledge of the savage act,
they salvaged innocence in public eyes
through purgative, inhuman rites that killed
the heinous, deformed beings they had borne.

Daemonic peddler of orgasmic dreams
deep within the hotbed sleep of wet desire,
brewed in cauldrons of medieval needs
banned antiquely by the Canon Law,
(which Bonaventure and Aquinas helped
define through rational resolve),
you leave a wake of dark despair,
the nevermore of normalcy in phantom lives.

LABYRINTH

Raucous,

out of sense

the thrashing about

in the maze

the bleating

thrusting out of depths,

the bellowing of passion
through the snout
nostrils flaring
like spouts for pain

Entrails of the beast
imprisoned in
the human cast of flesh
from which there is
no evolution
only extinction
into the Universe.

M I N O T A U R
is the surprise,
the unexpected
but desired End.

TRACKING THE MINOTAUR

We trudge to stone with listlessness

and climb the sides by clinging to inclines

that pyramid to heights with no depression.

We maze the solidarity to penetrate

and reach to core within incarceration

that trumps the mind's imagination.

We swerve avoiding the diluvian swell

and touch a depth against the soundings of our voice

that ricochet from granite breasts.

We trek in sand that sea has paralleled

and find in shells an echo of its wind

that has arisen in the desert dunes.

We wend through markers on an acute scale

and balance on a subterranean mean
that splits the vagueness into shafts.

We delve into submissiveness of thought
and preface all internment with farewells
that endings may not shatter into slivers.

We breach no barriers but the ones preset
and halt on coming to the fretted gate
that fear may have a place in heart.

We track our paths on difficult designs.

XII

LAND / SEA

"Before a blue sea filled with sirens stood the shade of Plato meditating ..."

"The harmony of the Greek language is the fragrance of the golden isles. Hellenic myths were born in the crystalline caves of mountains, in the verdant bosom of groves, in the blue landfalls of the sea. ... Homer the Patriarch is the voice of the golden isles."

THE GOLDEN ISLES

As old hexameters resound

with solar lust of gods and beasts,

and at the darkening of day,

when long-winged birds depart from marble ruins,

the wind resuscitates among last laurel trees

the calming murmur of Socratic fugues--

philosophy of stellar caste which transmigrated

out of myths and fables told relentlessly

within the span of man in time.

The tracks of the celestial bull

still lie upon the blue sea's edge.

The joyous songs are still becoming

in the shepherds' flutes of night.

ILLUSTRATIONS

: Dionysian revelers

: Dionysus

: Greek Krater of Dionysiac ritual: dismembering of a male by women

: Coin of Herakles with drawn bow

: Ikaros and Daedalus

: Images of Leucippus and Democritus, Greek Atomists

: Greek amphora

: Composite of the Greek Pantheon of Gods

: Zeus, c. 530-520 BCE, Dodona, Greece

: Hephaestus, God of Fire

: Goddesses—Eos, Diana, Hekate, Selene

: Entrance to a sacral cave on Crete

: "Medusa" by Leonardo Da Vinci

: Image of the Sun's rays

: Constellations, Hubble Telescope, NASA

: Event Horizon Telescope: Naked Singularity Projection, NASA

: "Orcus"

: Incubus ("The Nightmare") by Henri Fuseli. 1781

: "Incubus" Oil, 1789

: Gorgon on a Krater

: Labyrinth with Minotaur

: Minotaur Labyrinth Drachma, Crete, 330-300 BCE

: “Minotaur and Shadow” Photo by Samuel C. Sabean, 1954

: “Minotaur.” Classic image on a Krater

: The Celestial Bull Constellation

Statue of Valle-Inclán in Madrid, and author Robert Lima

ROBERT LIMA is a Cuban-born award-winning American poet, and was recognized internationally as a critic, bibliographer, playwright, and translator. As a Greenwich Village poet during the 1960s, he read at coffeehouses and other venues, co-edited *Seventh Street. Poems of Les Deux Megots*, introduced by Denise

Levertov, and the second series of *Judson Review*. His sixteen poetry collections include *Tracking the Minotaur, The Rites of Stone, Celestials, Elementals, Self, Sardinia/Sardegna, Ikons of the Past. Poetry of the Hispanic Americas, Writers on My Watch, and Odyssey* (2021). He has had exhibits of his framed poetry and visuals. Over 700 of his poems have appeared in print in the U.S. and abroad. Eleven of his poems appeared in Greek translation in *Noima Magazine*, published in Thessaloniki, Greece.

Among his numerous critical studies are books on García Lorca, Valle-Inclán, Borges, Surrealism, folklore, dramatic literature and translations of plays and poetry. He was invited and read his poetry for the archives at the Hispanic Division of The Library of Congress.

He was knighted by His Majesty King Juan Carlos I of Spain in 2003 and by the Prince of Borbón in 2017. He is listed in *Who's Who in the World* and other international directories.

RAMON DEL VALLE-INCLAN was born in 1866 in Vilanova de Arousa, Galicia, Spain. He was a member of the famed "Generación de 1898," which reassessed the condition of Spain upon the loss of its colonies after the Spanish-American War. He was a prolific author, producing twenty-four plays, twelve novels, four books of poetry and seven collections of stories, as well as numerous novelettes and articles in periodicals. As a playwright, he created a genre termed *Esperpento*, which depicts the absurdity and grotesquery of modern times, expressed most vividly in *Luces de bohemia* and *Divinas palabras*. In the novel, he created the memorable character the Marqués de Bradomín, protagonist of the four works titled Sonatas, and in a very different cast, the title character of *Tirano Banderas;* beyond these, he wrote novels of Spain's Carlist Wars, among others. He had a great impact on painters, writers, musicians, and others through his lifelong chats in the cafes of Madrid during which he expounded on his ideas on art, history, politics ... but his most important contribution was as an aesthetician. Many of the ideas of which he spoke in the cafe *tertulias* became the basis of his treatise *La lampara maravillosa* (1916), segments of which accompany the poetry in *Odyssey*. Valle-Inclán died in 1936 in the holy city of Santiago de Compostela. He did not live to see the *Esperpento* that was to be the Spanish Civil War.

Made in the USA
Middletown, DE
02 June 2021

40879879R10058